The Name of the Lord is...

Volume Four: From Aleph to Tav

By: Stephen Olar

The Name of the Lord is...

Other titles Available at Amazon.com

Bible Studies:

The Bible School Dropout's Bigger and Better Guide to Bible Study - Print and E-book editions available.

The Bible School Dropout's Guide to More Bible Study – Print and E-book editions available

The Bible School Dropout's Guide to Building the Word of God in My Life - Print and E-book editions available

The Bible School Dropout's Guide to Hebrews

The Bible School Dropout's Guide to Dispensationalism

The Bible School Dropout's Book of Charts

The Bible School Dropout's Guide to Genesis 1-11

The Bible School Dropout's Guide to Genesis 12-26

In Hot Pursuit: Twelve Things God Wants Us to Pursue – Print and E-Book versions.

Xtreme Xianity – Print and E-Book versions available

Core Elements – Print and E-book versions available

The Name of the Lord is… Volume One: Pretty Awesome, Great, Glorious and Like Totally Excellent! - Print and E-books versions available

The Name of the Lord is… Volume Two: Hi! I'm God - Print and E-book versions available

The Name of the Lord is… Volume 2.5: Hi! I'm still God. – Print and E-book versions available

The Name of the Lord is… Volume Three: The Great I Am - Print and E-books versions available

Novels:

Free – Print and E-book editions available

Icthus – Print and E-book editions available

Table of Contents

With a Little Help From my Friends

Welcome to volume four of our exploration of the Names of God. Well, technically it's the fifth book in this series when I decided to turn the study on combinations with Elohim and El into two study guides.

Although I started to gather material for this series many years ago, I have only concentrated on developing it into a series within the last two years. It has been challenging and rewarding study. It has stretched me as a writer as I have not really attempted a series of this scope before. It has also challenged me in my understanding of who God is.

One of the goals I had was to create a study which went beyond the more well-known names usually studied. Many Bible studies are designed to be completed in about two to three months. This makes it easier to plan small groups and Sunday school curriculum. This is also a popular topic and there is a lot of material out there. They range in formats from devotional, Bible study and full commentary.

Another goal has been to keep my opinion to a minimum. I have worked to design these studies in such a way you are not persuaded to come to the same conclusions I may have come to. I don't want to tell you what to believe about God's names and titles, but to give you the tools to discover them for yourself. I've in a few spoilers or suggestions, but I am also reasonably sure I haven't told you what to believe about the names you will explore. Well, haven't told you in most cases…

What has been really cool is several people have given me some classic works on the names of Christ and the names of God by Scholars such as Charles Roll and Herbert Lockyer. These have been some great resource material and I thank you for it.

Lockyer wrote many books which started with the word "all." When I was given *All the Divine Names and Titles in the Bible*, I realized I could write many more studies exploring this fascinating subject (Lockyer).

By the time you complete this study you will have explored more than 65 names and titles of God in the Old Testament. I say "about" because this current study is still a work in progress and may change a bit. There is one more planned study guide for this particular series on the Names and Titles of God in the New Testament.

You will also notice this book is called … from Aleph to Tav, which is the first and last letter of the Hebrew alphabet. It shouldn't take too long to realize the names are not in alphabetical order. Similar to the design of the other studies in the series I attempted to arrange them in the order they were first mentioned. A few of them, however, were placed in the study because the passage we examined was not necessarily the first mention but was a better example.

In this study we will be examining names and titles which did not seemed paired with Elohim or YAWEH. I put that word "seemed" deliberately because as this study developed I did discover some of them were paired. But that is the beauty of a study such as this. I've often compared Bible study to a treasure hunt. You never know what gems you will pick up along the way to examine.

The names listed in the lessons are transliterations of the Hebrew words. That's a fancy word indicating the Hebrew Word is a letter for letter translation to English. Depending on what source you use, you may find a difference in the spelling of the word. So thank you for not flooding my email with all the spelling errors you will find in the book. At least these ones because I am positive you will discover other spelling, typos, grammatical stuff and other formatting issues which my not-so-eagles eyes will have missed. Feedback is always welcome.

I will also be using the Déjà vu Review charts again for those names which we have already looked at it. Reviews are a good thing. Excessive redundancy is not.

Inductive Bible Study

Once again, I worked to design a study series which takes into consideration the principles of inductive Bible study. Three guidelines for this type of study are observation, interpretation and application. Each lesson contains elements which will allow you to follow the steps to reach your own conclusions. To help you in this goal, you will again discover a variety of charts and worksheets with each lesson.

Speaking of Charts…

One of the main concepts I worked with when I started doing these Bible studies was the idea of working step-by-step and focusing on one thing at a time and putting the pieces together as the information was collected and examined. The charts were designed as training tools to assist in the developing a systematic approach to studying any passage or topic. They have pretty much been a trademark in every study I've produced.

For more information on how to do Inductive Bible studies, please consult my other works; *The Bible School Dropout's Bigger and Better Guide to Bible Study* and *The Bible School Dropout's Guide to More Bible Study.*

E-Book Work Around

Many readers have left the paper world behind and have embrace e-books in a big way. I like e-books. I can have a huge library on my tablet and not in my office. It's also convenient and portable. If I am done with one book, I have another one to read with a couple of taps on the screen.

This study (and my other ones) is designed to be a workbook. You record your notes on the spaces and charts provided. Not so adaptable to an electronic format. A notebook will be required.

The second drawback of e-books is the page size, which adapts to the screen sized of the device. As a result, the charts, formatted for an 8x10 paper workbook, usually will not appear in one piece on an e-book reader. It tends to give the appearance the book is not properly formatted. It has been, but for a different format.

Enjoy Yourself

My last piece of advice before you dive into this study is to enjoy yourself.

Yes, Bible studies are times for thoughtful consideration of passages of Scripture which you want to discover what God has to say to you.

Yes, you should take your studying seriously.

Yes, you should be open to making the necessary changes in your life the Holy Spirit is prompting you to make as the end result of your study.

But this is not designed to be an in depth exploration of our topic. It may seem like that, but it's not. It is a snap shot of someone who wants us to know Him better by understanding what His names and titles mean.

However, if you look at like a chore to get through, you will not enjoy yourself and your Bible will end up serving as a place to put your TV remote on.

Ok! Let's get to it!

The Name of the Lord is...

Adonai – Lord

Talk about a brain fart. I was sure we had studied this name for God in a previous study. I even created a Déjà vu Review for it. The problem is I just couldn't find it. How can I lose a chapter of a book that is complete and published?

I don't know. It wasn't until after this study was a complete first draft and I was assembling it into the manuscript I found it. So I could leave this one out, but that would seem such a waste for both of us. When we looked at it in the other study (if you actually bought and did that study) it had been combined with YAWEH and was translated LORD God.

So I created this lesson. It answers with the question why some of our English versions sometimes refer to God as LORD and sometimes Lord.

Although there is a big hint in that statement, it is the only spoiler I'm going to give you.

Complete the Déjà vu Review for Adonai.

Read Genesis 15:1-6 and complete the Narrative Summary.

How is this word used in Scripture?

Is it a title which only applies to God?

How does Abram address God in this passage of Scripture?

Based on your understanding of this word why would Abram refer to God as "Lord?"

What is the main idea of this conversation?

What is did God promise in response to Abram's concerns?

The Name of the Lord is…

Depending on the version you are using, you may have noticed in verse 6 LORD is used instead of Lord. Find out what this word is?

How would you explain why Abram addressed God as Lord but the statement in verse six says "he believed in the LORD?"

How does Exodus 6:3 explain why Abram – later Abraham never addressed God as LORD?

Look up the following verses and complete the God Is/Does Chart. Look for at least five more verses and add your findings to the list.

Psalm 2:1-6	Job 28:28	Psalm 71:5	Psalm 86:15
Isaiah 6:8	Isaiah 11:11	Lamentations 3:58	Daniel 9:15-19

What did you discover about the word Adonai in reference to God?

Complete the My Name Is chart?

Complete the following phrase:

I acknowledge God as Adonai because…

Déjà vu Review

Adonai = Lord, God

Strong's #: 136	Word:	Definition:

Verses:

The Name of the Lord Is... Volume 3: The Great I am, Page 159

What did I discover about this name?

Narrative Summary

Date of Study:

Passage:	Title:

Type of narration: Story, Account, Chronology, Information, Backfill

Characters:	Theme:

Details:	Support

Principles:	Illustrates:

Summary:

Takeaway:

God Is/Does

Reference	Description	What do I think it means?	Support

My Name Is: Date:

First Mention:	Title:

Strong's #:	Definition:
Times Used:	

Other Sources	Notes/Definitions

Scripture	How Used	Support

Insight

Takeaway

Additional Notes:

Déjà vu Review

Shaddai = Almighty

Strong's #: 7706	Word:	Definition:

Verses:

Job 11:7 - "Can you search out the deep things of God?
Can you find out the limits of the Almighty?

The Name of the Lord is… Volume 2: Hi! I'm God. Page 55

What did I discover about this name?

Volume 4: From Aleph to Tav

Shawphat – Judge

It is interesting to see how some words are used to describe God. Would it surprise you to learn this is actually a verb, and yet it is used as a title or name of God? Since we have seen this several times it shouldn't be.

I am amazed at this particular use of the word. When we think of judges we think of justice. A somber court room, a person residing on a raised platform, dressed in black robes. He weighs the evidence and issues a verdict.

But this word has a different meaning. I could tell you want it is, but why spoil the fun of discovering that for yourself?

Let's begin our study by examining the word. Please complete the Word Summary for H8199.

What did you discover about this word?

What is the alternate meaning for this word?

Why is that significant?

Now let's read Genesis 18:16-33 and complete the Narrative Summary for this passage.

Who are the people in this passage conversing?

What is the conversation about?

P a g e | 19

The Name of the Lord is...

What is the full title Abraham calls God?

What is the significance of this title?

Consider the following verses in context and complete the God Is/Does Chart.

1 Samuel 12:7	Psalm 75:7	Psalm 96:13
Psalm 43:1	Psalm 82:8	Isaiah 33:22
Psalm 50:6	Psalm 94:12	Isaiah 51:5

Do a Scripture search and add at least 5 verses to the God Is/Does Chart.

What did you learn about The Judge of the Earth?

Complete the My Name is Chart.

Finish the following phrase:

I can place my confidence in Shawphat because...

Word Summary

Date of Study:

Word:	Verse:
Strong's Number:	
Definition:	
Times Used:	

Other Sources	Definition(s)

Other Bible References	How Used

Putting it My Own Words

Takeaway

Narrative Summary

Date of Study:

Passage:		Title:	

Type of narration: Story, Account, Chronology, Information, Backfill

Characters:	Theme:

Details:	Support

Principles:	Illustrates:

Summary:

Takeaway:

God Is/Does

Reference	Description	What do I think it means?	Support

My Name Is:　　　　Date:

First Mention:	Title:
Strong's #:	Definition:
Times Used:	

Other Sources	Notes/Definitions

Scripture	How Used	Support

Insight

Takeaway

Additional Notes:

The Name of the Lord is...

Eheyeh ashair Eheyeh – I Am Who I Am

Moses mind was already reeling from his personal encounter with God in the form of the burning bush. God wasn't interested in only revealing Himself to Moses. He had a mission for the humble shepherd, formerly a prince of Egypt. God wanted to use Moses as the instrument to lead Israel out of bondage.

He felt totally inadequate for the job. But God had chosen His man to carry out the plan and wasn't going to take "no" for an answer.

Moses was probably aware of the stories about the God of his ancestors; Abraham, Isaac, and Jacob and the promises which were made to them. But he was still thinking of ways to turn down the offer. I know – I'm being nice. God wasn't offering Moses a job; He was calling Moses to be the leader of a fledgling nation.

Moses, who did not have much experience at that time in conversing with this being and asked the question, "And how am I to introduce You to these people (my paraphrase)?"

God's answer has puzzled theologians and Bible students ever since: "I AM who I AM. Tell then I AM sent you."

"So I'm supposed to tell the elders and leaders of the community some voice coming from a burning bush called Himself 'I AM' sent me?"

Well, I would have asked that question. I'm a little surprised Moses gave it a pass. After all he was the one looking for an exit plan. Perhaps it was the whole burning bush thing. Perhaps he was thinking of the other questions which would arise from the elders. Such as, "And what were you smoking at the time? Yeah, right… burning bush…rod to a snake…"

Generally, many of the commentators I've consulted considered this phrase/name helps define YAWEH (Self-existent One or Eternal One). The use of Eheyeh serves to emphasize several characteristics of God which include…

Yeah – like I'm going to just tell you.

Complete the Word Summary for H1961.

What did you discover about this word?

The Name of the Lord is...

Read Exodus 3:12-22 and complete the Narrative Summary for this passage.

What is context of this passage?

Why do you think Moses asked God what His name was?

What is significant about how God identified Himself as the God of Abraham, Isaac and Jacob? There is a hint found in Luke 20:37-38. The other hint can be found in Genesis 17:1-7.

What does God promise to do in this passage?

What does God say about His name?

What passage in the New Testament identifies Jesus as Eheyeh?

Complete the My Name is Summary.

What did you learn about Eheyeh ashair Eheyeh from your study?

What characteristics of God do Eheyeh ashair Eheyeh show us? Just because I gave you space for five answers, don't assume there are only six. You may find less or more. If you promise me not to peek, I will include my answers under the Additional Notes section for this chapter. No peeking, however, until you have provided your own answers.

1.

2.

3.

4.

5.

6.

Complete the following phrase:

I can have complete confidence in Eheyeh because...

Word Summary

Date of Study:

Word:	Verse:
Strong's Number:	
Definition:	
Times Used:	

Other Sources	Definition(s)

Other Bible References	How Used

Putting it My Own Words

Takeaway

Narrative Summary

Date of Study:

Passage:	Title:

Type of narration: Story, Account, Chronology, Information, Backfill

Characters:	Theme:

Details:	Support

Principles:	Illustrates:

Summary:

Takeaway:

My Name Is:

Date:

First Mention:	Title:
Strong's #:	**Definition:**
Times Used:	

Other Sources	Notes/Definitions

Scripture	How Used	Support

Insight

Takeaway

Additional Notes:

This is the list of the characteristics I think Eheyeh ashair Eheyeh demonstrate.

1. Self-existence

2. Eternal

3. Unchangeable

4. Incomprehensible

5. Faithful

6. True

The Name of the Lord is…

Tsur Yeshooaw – The Rock of Salvation

This is one of those names which I had to make a judgment call on. We've studied both words in conjunction with Elohim or YAWEH. So I suppose I could have gotten away with a Déjà vu Review. That option rolled around in my brain for about three quarters of second.

Once I started examining this name of God, I was once again reminded how the prize is often under the surface.

Let's remind ourselves of Tsur and Yeshooaw by completing the Déjà vu reviews.

Now take a look at a new word and complete the Word Summary for H3444.

How does H3444 add to our understanding of the word translated as salvation?

Read Deuteronomy 32.

In the Context of this passage how is The Rock of His Salvation used?

List the how God is described in this chapter as well as what He did for the nation.

How do these descriptions apply to the Rock of his Salvation?

The Name of the Lord is...

Read 2 Samuel 22: 44-51 and complete the Poetry Summary for this passage.

What is the context of this passage?

Why did David refer to God as the Rock of My Salvation?

For the next two questions complete the Comparison chart.

Go back to the beginning of 2 Samuel 22 and take a look at verses 1-7. Record the names he calls God and the reasons he gave for this song of praise.

Much of this passage is repeated in Psalm 18. If you read verses 31-50 record any names and the reasons he gives for this praise. Note if this passage sounds familiar, it is... You studied it in passage Volume 2.5. Well, at least I hoped you studied it.

What are the similarities?

What are the differences?

What do you think is significant about the differences?

Read the following passages and complete the God Is/Does chart

Psalm 62

Psalm 71:1-7 – Spoiler… Tsur is not translated rock in this passage; at least not in the NKJV. Make a note of what word is translated rock.

Psalm 89: 26 – How does the author introduce the Psalm?

How does this relate to the name we are studying?

What did you learn about the Rock of My Salvation?

Complete the My Name Is chart.

Finish this statement.

God, you are the Rock of My Salvation for the following reasons.

Déjà vu Review

Tsur = Rock		
Strong's #: 6697	Word:	Definition:

Verses:
2 Samuel 22: 47

The Name of the Lord is... Volume 2.5: Hi! I'm Still God. Page 107

What did I discover about this name?

Déjà vu Review

Salvation/Saviour		
Strong's #: 3468	Word:	Definition:

Verses:
Psalm 18:46

The Name of the Lord is... Volume 2.5: Hi! I'm Still God. Page 67
What did I discover about this name?

Word Summary   Date of Study:

Word:	Verse:
Strong's Number:	
Definition:	
Times Used:	

Other Sources	Definition(s)

Other Bible References	How Used

Putting it My Own Words

Takeaway

Poetry Summary

Date of Study:

Passage	Title:
Historical Context:	

Verse:	Images:	Support

Insight from the Context:

Insight from Other Scripture or Sources	Source

Takeaway:

Comparison Summary

vs.

	Scripture	

Insight:

Takeaway:

God Is/Does

Reference	Description	What do I think it means?	Support

My Name Is: Date:

First Mention:	Title:
Strong's #:	**Definition:**
Times Used:	

Other Sources	Notes/Definitions

Scripture	How Used	Support

Insight

Takeaway

Additional Notes:

The Name of the Lord is...

Awsaw - Maker

We have previously discovered a word translated into English may come from more than one Hebrew word. There are three words which have all been translated as Maker in reference to God. For me, this challenged my English understanding of what Maker means.

I thought this was similar to another word we discovered, bara, which means creator. However there are some subtle and distinct differences and makes it worth spending a little time exploring the concepts suggested by these words used to describe the same person.

1. Awsaw

Please complete the Word Summary for H6213.

What did you discover about this word as it refers to God?

Read Job 4 to get an idea of the context of how this word is used here. Complete the Narrative and Didactical Summaries to discern the logical course of the discussion.

What is the basis for Eliphaz's argument he his using to explain as the cause for Job's suffering?

This particular word is used twice more in Job. Take a look at them and determine if the use of this word is consistent with what you have already discovered. Please explain in a sentence or two

Job 32 (22)

Job 35 (10)

The Name of the Lord is...

Look up the following verses and record your findings on the God Is/Does chart. Remember to consider the context of the passage the verse is in.

Psalm 95:6   Proverbs 22:2   Isaiah 51:13   Isaiah 54:5

What ideas does the use of this word give you about God?

Here is some value added information to consider. The Complete Word Study Dictionary; Old Testament fleshed out the usage of this word by indicating the context of this word tends to indicate an activity with a "distinct purpose, moral obligation or goal in mind (Baker, The Complete Word Study Dictionary; Old Testament).

Does this change your conclusions regarding this word and how?

2. Pawal

Only translate once as Maker, this word is used in describing the works God has done. So let's take a look at how it is used and some of the things God has done.

Complete the Word Summary for H6466.

What did you discover about this word?

Read Job 36:1-12.

This is a continuation of Elihu's discourse on his reasons Job has been afflicted which we already touched upon. How this word different than the first word used?

Examine the following verses and add your findings to the God Is/Does Chart.

Exodus 15:17	Psalm 68:28	Proverbs 16:4	Isaiah 26:12
Isaiah 41:4	Zephaniah 2:3		

How do these verses add to your understanding of the Maker?

3. Yatsar

When I explored this word I discovered another concept of the Maker which added to my understanding of the greatness of God in the scheme of things. When you examine this word think "potter" or "sculptor."

Complete the Word Summary for H3335.

What did you learn about this word?

Read Psalm 95 and complete the Poetry Summary. Please note two of the three words we are examining in this lesson appear in this Psalm.

What is the theme of this Psalm?

According to Psalm 95 what did God make?

Look up the following references and add your findings to the God Is/Does Chart.

Genesis 2:7	Psalm 2:9	Psalm 139:16	Isaiah 45:9-12
Jeremiah 1:5			

The Name of the Lord is...

How does this word add to your understanding of God as Maker?

Complete the My Name is Chart.

What did you discover about God as the Maker which you may not have been aware of before?

Complete the following statement.

I acknowledge and bow my knee to my Maker for the following reasons...

Word Summary

Date of Study:

Word:	Verse:
Strong's Number:	
Definition:	
Times Used:	

Other Sources	Definition(s)

Other Bible References	How Used

Putting it My Own Words

Takeaway

Didactical Summary

Date of Study:

Passage:		Title		
Author:		Thesis:		
Audience:				
Verse	Argument	Statement		Support

Insight

Takeaway

Word Summary

Date of Study:

Word:	Verse:
Strong's Number:	
Definition:	
Times Used:	

Other Sources	Definition(s)

Other Bible References	How Used

Putting it My Own Words

Takeaway

Word Summary   Date of Study:

Word:	Verse:
Strong's Number:	

Definition:

Times Used:

Other Sources	Definition(s)

Other Bible References	How Used

Putting it My Own Words

Takeaway

Poetry Summary

Date of Study:

Passage	Title:	
Historical Context:		
Verse:	**Images:**	**Support**
Insight from the Context:		
Insight from Other Scripture or Sources		**Source**
Takeaway:		

God Is/Does

Reference	Description	What do I think it means?	Support

My Name Is:

Date:

First Mention:	Title:
Strong's #:	**Definition:**
Times Used:	

Other Sources	Notes/Definitions

Scripture	How Used	Support

Insight

Takeaway

Additional Notes:

Déjà vu Review

Deliverer		
Strong's #: 6403	Word:	Definition:

Verses:
Psalm 18:2

The name of the Lord Is: Vol. 3 – page 95
What did I discover about this name?

The Name of the Lord is...

Nawtsar Awdawm- Watcher of Men

This little Gem of a name is only used once in the Old Testament. But it has multiple facets which help us to understand a bit of how God works in the lives of men. We find Job used this name when he asked some very significant questions in the midst of his suffering.

Back then, like today there is a tendency to think wealth, power and position are the blessings of God and the lack of them indicates a person has sinned and is cursed of God. Job, who feels he is alone and not comforted in his time of sorrow asks Nawtsar Awdawm "Have I sinned?" And "What have I done to You, that you have painted a target on my back?" .

What hasn't changed in the centuries since those questions were asked is nothing. When we come to the subject of suffering and sin we are sitting with Job just as perplexed.

Now I don't want you to get locked into an early assumption of what the name is associated with. Make sure you investigate how this word is used before you come to any conclusions.

I found it interesting there is a wide variation of how this word is translated in various English versions. This is my spoiler for this lesson. Below are several Versions and how Nawtsar Awdawm was translated.

NKVJ Watcher of Men	KJV Preserver of Men	NIV You who see everything we do	NASB Watcher of Men
AMP Watcher of mankind	NOG You insist on spying on people	MSG You're responsible for every human being	VOICE You who watch after humanity

Now that I've got you thinking about this name let's start where we usually do. Please complete the Word Summaries for H5341 and H120.

What are the different meanings for Nawtsar?

Using the website www.biblegateway.com, another multiple version website, or program such as E-Sword, make a list of eight versions and how these words were translated. And no, you cannot use the ones I've already listed.

The Name of the Lord is…

Version	Translation	Version	Translation

How do these various translations add to your understanding of who Nawtsar Awdawm is?

Examine the following verses and complete the God Is/Does chart.

Proverbs 22:12   Psalm 32:7   Psalm 140:4   Isaiah 42:6
Psalm 12:7   Psalm 40:11   Isaiah 27:3   Isaiah 49:8

What do these verses tell us about what God does?

What did you learn about God through the name Nawtsar Awdawm?

Complete the My Name is chart.

Finish the following statement

Nawtsar Awdawm, the Watcher of Men, is my keeper and guardian because

Word Summary

Date of Study:

Word:	Verse:
Strong's Number:	
Definition:	
Times Used:	

Other Sources	Definition(s)

Other Bible References	How Used

Putting it My Own Words

Takeaway

Word Summary   Date of Study:

Word:	Verse:
Strong's Number:	
Definition:	
Times Used:	

Other Sources	Definition(s)

Other Bible References	How Used

Putting it My Own Words

Takeaway

God Is/Does

Reference	Description	What do I think it means?	Support

My Name Is:

Date:

First Mention:	Title:
Strong's #:	**Definition:**
Times Used:	

Other Sources	Notes/Definitions

Scripture	How Used	Support

Insight

Takeaway

Additional Notes:

The Name of the Lord is...

Melek – King

When we think of kings we think of power and authority. The good thing about this word is it used a lot. I am not going to pretend I have looked at every passage where this word refers to God. It would make for a really long study. The Hebrew version of the word is used over 2500 times. The Aramaic version is used another 181 times. This was the language spoken by those people who had been taken into exile by the Babylonians.

I am surprised we haven't seen this word in combination with Elohim or YAWEH, but then with so many places to look I wouldn't be surprised if somewhere in the Old Testament it turns up. I call it serendipity.

Complete the Word Summary for H4428. The Aramaic version is H4430. Since the both mean the same thing it is not necessary to define that word...unless you want to – I know you want to.

Were there any surprises when you defined this word? What were they and why did you find it a surprise?

Read Psalm 5 and complete the Poetry Summary.

Why does David call God My King in this passage?

What other names does he call God and why?

What are all the things David acknowledges God for?

The Name of the Lord is...

Based on your understanding of the word melek, why do you think David referred to God as his king?

Look up the following verses and record your findings in the God Is/Does Chart. Using your resources, look up five more verses and record what you discover about God as King. Remember to consider the context of the passages you examine

Psalm 24:7   Psalm 47:7   Psalm 89:18   Isaiah 41:21
Daniel 4:37   Hosea 13:10

According to the passages you have examined who does God have authority over?

What conclusions did you reach as you studied this word in relation to God?

Complete the My Name is Chart?

Complete the following thought.

I acknowledge God to be my King for the following reasons.

Word Summary   Date of Study:

Word:	Verse:
Strong's Number:	
Definition:	
Times Used:	

Other Sources	Definition(s)

Other Bible References	How Used

Putting it My Own Words

Takeaway

God Is/Does

Reference	Description	What do I think it means?	Support

My Name Is:

Date:

First Mention:	Title:

Strong's #:	Definition:
Times Used:	

Other Sources	Notes/Definitions

Scripture	How Used	Support

Insight

Takeaway

Additional Notes:

Meginaw – My Shield

The first three verses of Psalm 18 are a real treasure in exploring the names and titles of God. It took some time to sort out which ones we have explored before and which ones are new. Six of them should be familiar if you have been working through this series. They are:

Strong's Number	Word	Translated As	Meaning	Reference
H6697	Tsur	Strength	A cliff or rock or refuge	The Name of the Lord is... Vol 2.5, page 107
H5553	Sela	Rock	A craggy rock, fortress or stronghold	The Name of the Lord is... Vol 2.5, page 107
H6403	Pawlat	Deliverer	Carry away safe, deliver, cause to escape	The Name of the Lord is... Vol. 3, page107
H3068	YAWEH	LORD	God's name	The Name of the Lord is... Vol. 3, page 13
H410	Elohim	God	God	The Name of the Lord is... Vol 2, page 9
H4686	Mawstood	Fortress	Fortress, castle, stronghold	The Name of the Lord is... Vol. 3, page 87

There are two words which we haven't studied, but we have looked at other words which have the same or similar meanings.

Word From the Passage				Word We Have Studied Before			
Strong's Number	Word	Translated as	Meaning	Strong's Number	Word	Translated as	Reference
H2391	Kayzek	Strength	Strength	H5797	Oz	Strength	Vol. 2.5, page97
H4869	Misgaeb	High Tower	Cliff, defense or tower	H4206	Migdawl	Tower, castle	Vol 1, page 87

That leaves two words to explore. Hold that thought, I'll come back to them in a couple of paragraphs.

In order to prevent a lot of redundant studies in this and the last study guide, I created a review chart (Déjà vu Review) for the words we have studied before and sprinkled them throughout the guides. Occasionally I put them into a lesson when it was related to the specific study. But to throw six of them into one lesson would make it too confusing, long and awkward and putting them throughout the guide too much review. I really wouldn't make you repeatedly hunt for them in order to complete this study, which I think most of you would find frustrating.

I mean, think about it. You now have three other studies to refer to – if you actually bought and did them. Not only am I asking you to refer to these guides to complete the reviews I would have also had you flipping through this guide like an old magazine at the doctor's office.

You're welcome.

Now that is not to say you will not see some of these names appear as reviews in other guides – reviewing is usually a good thing. I thought it would not work well in this particular instance. To make our study more streamlined and focused I decided to mention those words we don't need to restudy. I am including our synonyms here as well.

Let's return to the two remaining names. We will be exploring My Shield in this lesson and The Horn of my Salvation in the following lesson.

The question to answer at the end of our explorations is this: What do all these words have in common when used in the first three verses of Psalm 18 and what applications can we draw from them?

Let's get stated by completing the Word Summary for H4043

What definitions did you find out for this word? Make a note if the meaning is literal or figurative.

What is the purpose of a shield?

Read Psalm 18 and complete the Poetry Summary for the first three verses.

Where else in Scripture is this Psalm recorded?

Complete the Comparison chart on the two passages of Scripture. For now refer only to the passages which correspond to the first three verses of Psalm 18. You do not have to the entire Psalm. You are certainly free to study the complete Psalm, and I encourage you to do so, but for this lesson, we are focusing only on the first three verses.

What differences did you observe?

How do you think these differences relate to the rest of this passage?

Look at other passages where this word is used. You have 63 verses to choose from. Locate five references which seem to refer to God being a shield and record your findings on the God Is/Does chart. Although I only asked for five, locating more will give you a bigger picture of why God is called a shield.

Complete the My Name is Chart

What did you learn about My Shield?

Complete this thought:

You, My God are my shield because…

Word Summary   Date of Study:

Word:	Verse:
Strong's Number:	

Definition:

Times Used:

Other Sources	Definition(s)

Other Bible References	How Used

Putting it My Own Words

Takeaway

Poetry Summary

Date of Study:

Passage	Title:	
Historical Context:		
Verse:	**Images:**	**Support**
Insight from the Context:		
Insight from Other Scripture or Sources		**Source**
Takeaway:		

Comparison Summary

vs.

	Scripture	

Insight:

Takeaway:

God Is/Does

Reference	Description	What do I think it means?	Support

My Name Is:

Date:

First Mention:	Title:
Strong's #:	Definition:
Times Used:	

Other Sources	Notes/Definitions

Scripture	How Used	Support

Insight

Takeaway

Additional Notes:

The Name of the Lord is...

Keren Yeshah – Horn of my Salvation

I really enjoyed my time studying this name. It brought to mind those old western movies where the wagons are circled, under attack, and there appears to be no hope. Then in the distance you hear the bugle call of the cavalry coming to the rescue – Deus ex Machina at some of its corniest and unbelievable moments (Outside help "suddenly" appears and saves the hero.).

In Scripture a horn refers to many several things. Most obvious is an animal horn. Then you are thinking of a musical instrument it was most often created from an animal horn (think shophar). It was used to call people to order, sound the attack or retreat and the start of some Jewish festivals.

The corners of the altar were also called horns. People seeking mercy from enemies would often run to the tabernacle or temple and grasp the horns of the altar, where they would be safe until their guilt or innocence could be determined. Some of the sacrifices also required the priests to sprinkle the horns of the altar with the blood of the animal.

So we have three concepts in particular which may or may not fit the context of this passage and an idea of how this word is used – mercy, rescue and sacrifice. The answer could be one or a combination of the three ideas. That is for you to decide at the conclusion of your exploration.

We have already examined one of the words in this name; salvation. Please turn to the lesson on Rock of Salvation if wish to review it.

Please complete the Word Summary for H3468.

What are the definitions which could be applied to this verse? Think of literal and figurative usages of the word. Include at least one Scripture reference for each definition.

What was also applied to the horns of the altar and why?

Where is the phrase "horn of salvation" used elsewhere in the Bible? For each reference, write one sentence or two if you need to, on how this phrase is used. (Hint: there is at least one reference in the New Testament.)

What do you think the significance is of The Horn of My Salvation when applied to God?

Review your notes on the previous lesson on My Shield.

From your notes, why did David write Psalm 18?

Record each name and title you find in Psalm 18 on the Find the Connection Chart and indicate if it refers to an offensive or defensive action or position on the part of David. Also provide a reason why you think it is offensive or defensive. Use all the passages you have examined in these two studies.

Why is it important to understand it is God who defends, protects, shields and gives us strength when we face our enemies?

David was saved from his enemies, primarily Saul. Who would qualify as the enemies God saves us from?

Complete the My Name Is chart.

How would you finish the following statement?

I recognize God is the Horn of My Salvation for the following reason (s).

Word Summary   Date of Study:

Word:	Verse:
Strong's Number:	
Definition:	
Times Used:	

Other Sources	Definition(s)

Other Bible References	How Used

Putting it My Own Words

Takeaway

Find the Connection

Passage	Name/Title	Offensive or Defensive	Why?

My Name Is: Date:

First Mention:	Title:
Strong's #:	**Definition:**
Times Used:	

Other Sources	Notes/Definitions

Scripture	How Used	Support

Insight

Takeaway

Additional Notes:

Gibbor – Mighty One

In another lesson I mentioned (or will mention depending on the final order of the lessons) discovering new stuff during the course of a Bible study as serendipity. A standard definition of serendipity is "an aptitude for making desirable discoveries by accident (http://www.dictionary.com/browse/serendipity?s=t)." When I first came across this word it was by itself so it ended up in this volume of the series.

In previous guides we looked at Mighty God and Mighty God of Israel. I developed two lessons because there were two words to explore. So I thought this is a good thing – a quick review and on to the next word.

It appeared not to be the case. This was a new word to explore. So I worked on this study and based it on Psalm 45.

At least that was the plan. When I started exploring this word in greater detail I learned a couple of different things. The first is I found it appears to be a compound name which appeared in an earlier volume (2.5 to be exact) on The Great God. The second discovery was seemed to be used conjunction another word or two. The irony of that statement is the previous study was based on Nehemiah 9…which is mentioned in this study.

Sigh.

It seems redundant to study this name twice, but I had this nice little study sitting on my computer looking for a home. But that is where serendipity kicks in. In the end it was a pleasant discovery to explore a different facet of this gem.

Complete Déjà vu Review for H 1368.

Read Psalm 45 and complete the Poetry Summary.

What is the main theme of this Psalm?

How does this Psalm depict God as a warrior?

How else is God described in this passage?

The Name of the Lord is…

According to the context who is the bride?

Why would it be important to view a king mighty, strong, or a warrior?

Read the following passages and record your findings in the God Is/Does chart. Remember to consider the context of the passage.

Deuteronomy 10:17   Nehemiah 9.32   Psalm 24:8   Isaiah 10:20-22
Isaiah 42:13   Jeremiah 20:11   Jeremiah 32:17-19 Zephaniah 3:17

Did you discover the two words which seemed to also be associated with mighty in reference to God? I did give you a hint. Check out H3372 and H1419.

What did you discover about God as the Mighty One which added to your understanding of who God is and what He does?

Complete the My Name is Chart.

In my life He is Gibbor, the Mighty One because…

Déjà vu Review

Gibbor = Mighty One		
Strong's #: H1368	Word:	Definition:

Verses:

Psalm 45:

Then Name of the Lord is... Volume 2.5, page 49

What did I discover about this name?

Poetry Summary   Date of Study:

Passage	Title:
Historical Context:	

Verse:	Images:	Support

Insight from the Context:

Insight from Other Scripture or Sources	Source

Takeaway:

God Is/Does

Reference	Description	What do I think it means?	Support

My Name Is:

Date:

First Mention:	Title:
Strong's #:	Definition:
Times Used:	

Other Sources	Notes/Definitions

Scripture	How Used	Support

Insight

Takeaway

Additional Notes:

The Name of the Lord is...

Kawdesh Yisrael - Holy One of Israel

This is one of those names which I considered not including it in the study. In previous studies we explored the concepts of the Holy God, the God of Israel and the LORD who Sanctifies. I thought about only doing a Deja View Review on it and move on.

When I studied this word more, I was curious about something. Almost all of the references I located regarding his name are found in Isaiah with the exceptions of one in the Psalms and Ezekiel. Since most reference were written by prophets the question arises as to if what they had to say already came to pass or is still waiting fulfilment.

In my investigations I also came across one reference to the Holy One of Jacob (also in Isaiah). I included in this lesson due to the fact Jacob and Israel are often used interchangeably.

The second question I had was to decide if this is a reference to Jesus Christ and should be filed for when I would start on that study. When you have completed this study, you may come to a similar conclusion.

So after considering the options and angle, I flipped an imaginary coin and put it here. So let's start our study not with examining our words, but with a review of one of the words (Israel is rather self-explanatory). Please complete the Deja View Review for the word *Holy*.

Read Psalm 71 and complete the Poetry Summary.

What is this Psalm about?

How is God described and why?

What is the psalmist's response in verses 22-24?

Read Isaiah 29:17-24 and complete the Prophecy Worksheet.

What is this passage referring to?

The Name of the Lord is...

Has this event already been fulfilled? I don't want you to slap down a one word answer. Give up a sentence or two or three to explain your reasoning.

What clues do you find in the passage this is still a future event?

Read Isaiah 43:1-7 and complete the Prophecy Worksheet.

What is this passage about?

What is God doing in this passage?

What evidence from this passage indicates we are still waiting for its fulfillment?

Examine the following verses. Yes, even the ones you have already looked at and complete the God Is/Does chart.

Holy One of Jacob
Isaiah 29:23
Holy One of Israel
Psalm 71:22   Isaiah 43:3   Isaiah 55:5   Isaiah 60:9   Isaiah 60:14
Ezekiel 39:7

What did you learn about God from these passages which you may have not known before?

Complete the My Name Is Chart.

Finish the following statement.

I bow the knee to the Holy One of Israel for the following reasons:

Déjà vu Review		
Holy One		
Strong's #: 6918	Word:	Definition:
Verses:		
Job 6:10		
Habakkuk 1:12		
Habakkuk 3:3		
Isaiah 43:15		
The Name of the Lord is: Vol 2.5 – page 145		
What did I discover about this name?		

Poetry Summary   Date of Study:

Passage	Title:	
Historical Context:		

Verse:	Images:	Support

Insight from the Context:	

Insight from Other Scripture or Sources	Source

Takeaway:

Prophecy

Date of Study:

Passage:	Title:
Speaker:	Audience
Fulfilled? ☐ yes ☐ no when Fulfilled:	Thesis:

Literal:	Support

Figures/Symbols	Represents	Support

Passage in Context:

Purpose(s) of the Prophecy:

Takeaway:

Prophecy

Date of Study:

Passage:	Title:
Speaker:	Audience
Fulfilled? ☐ yes ☐ no when Fulfilled:	Thesis:

Literal:		Support

Figures/Symbols	Represents	Support

Passage in Context:

Purpose(s) of the Prophecy:

Takeaway:

God Is/Does

Reference	Description	What do I think it means?	Support

My Name Is: Date:

First Mention:	Title:	
Strong's #:	Definition:	
Times Used:		

Other Sources	Notes/Definitions

Scripture	How Used	Support

Insight

Takeaway

Additional Notes:

Bara – Creator

What is the meaning of life?

This question has challenged the purpose of humanity almost from the time of creation. Solomon, one of the wisest men who ever lived, addressed it from his unique perspective in his discourse in Ecclesiastes.

He was a man gifted with God-given wisdom. This wisdom brought him fame, wealth and power like few have ever seen. Yet in the end he realized this was nothing when compared to eternity.

When we look at the English word Creator in Ecclesiastes 12 the tendency is to assume it is a noun. Yet like many of the names we have studied in previous lessons, it is in fact a verb. It is the same word from Genesis 1:1; "In the beginning God created the heavens and the earth."

Another interesting aspect of this word is of the 53 times it is used in the Old Testament about 47 times, more or less, God is the subject. Mull those around a bit while you are exploring The Creator.

Let's start were we usually start. Please complete the Word Summary for H1254.

What did you discover about this word?

Read Ecclesiastes 12 and complete the Poetry Summary for Verses 1-7.

When does he urge us to remember our Creator?

What is he describing in this passage?

The Name of the Lord is…

What does he have to say about wisdom in verses 8-12

What is his conclusion to the entire message in verses 13-14?

Why should we fear God and obey His commandments?

Look up the following passages and complete the God Is/Does Chart. Using a concordance or similar study aid, do a search and add at least five more verses which talk about God creating or as Creator.

Genesis 1:1   Psalm 145:8   Isaiah 40:25-28   Isaiah 43:14-15

Isaiah 45:7-8   Deuteronomy 4:32   Psalm 51:10   Isaiah 65:17-18

What insights did you learn from your exploration of these passages?

Complete the My Name Is Chart.

Complete the following thought:

I will remember my Creator because…

Word Summary   Date of Study:

Word:	Verse:
Strong's Number:	
Definition:	
Times Used:	

Other Sources	Definition(s)

Other Bible References	How Used

Putting it My Own Words

Takeaway

Poetry Summary

Date of Study:

Passage	Title:

Historical Context:

Verse:	Images:	Support

Insight from the Context:

Insight from Other Scripture or Sources	Source

Takeaway:

God Is/Does

Reference	Description	What do I think it means?	Support

My Name Is: Date:

First Mention:	Title:
Strong's #:	**Definition:**
Times Used:	

Other Sources	Notes/Definitions

Scripture	How Used	Support

Insight

Takeaway

Additional Notes:

The Name of the Lord is...

Kawkak – Lawgiver

All right... All right, I could have put this word in the study with YAWEH (LORD). But in my defense I wasn't aware of this name when that study guide was written. It may have also meant two volumes for name combinations with YAWEH. It is also one of those names or titles where it is only used once in Isaiah 33.

When I first look up the meaning of the word I had to double check my Strong's Number because it wasn't what I expected it to be. But then when I thought about the contextual usage of it I realized it made sense. It seemed appropriate because it reminded me of God on Mount Sinai when He gave the Law to Moses.

The basic meaning of the word is...

Did you actually think I would give you that information? You silly person...

Pull out your Strong's and complete the Word Summary for H2710.

What was your impression when you first examined the definitions of this word?

Read Isaiah 33:13-24 and complete the Prophetic and Didactical Summaries.

What is this prophecy about?

Do you think this prophecy been fulfilled partially or completely? Explain your answer.

The Name of the Lord is...

Refer to your notes from the Didactical Summary and show the argument which is made in this passage.

What is the main argument here?

What does God want the people to know?

There are two other names attached to YAWEH in verse 22. What is the significance of them in this passage?

Judge (H8199)

King (H4428)

How does the Lawgiver fit into this mix?

Complete the My Name is Chart.

What did you learn about the Lawgiver which you may have not known before?

Complete the following phrase.

I acknowledge the YAWEH to be the Lawgiver because...

Word Summary
Date of Study:

Word:	Verse:
Strong's Number:	
Definition:	
Times Used:	

Other Sources	Definition(s)

Other Bible References	How Used

Putting it My Own Words

Takeaway

Prophecy

Date of Study:

Passage:	**Title:**
Speaker:	**Audience**
Fulfilled? ☐ yes ☐ no **when Fulfilled:**	**Thesis:**

Literal:	**Support**

Figures/Symbols	**Represents**	**Support**

Passage in Context:

Purpose(s) of the Prophecy:

Takeaway:

Didactical Summary

Date of Study:

Passage:		Title		
Author:		Thesis:		
Audience:				
Verse	**Argument**	**Statement**		**Support**

Insight

Takeaway

My Name Is: Date:

First Mention:	Title:
Strong's #:	**Definition:**
Times Used:	

Other Sources	Notes/Definitions

Scripture	How Used	Support

Insight

Takeaway

Additional Notes:

The Name of the Lord is…

Bawal – Husband

I included this title for God because it speaks of the intimate relationship God has with Israel. In the New Testament the Church is described as the Bride of Christ and there may be some correlation, but please keep in mind there is a difference between the two.

Like all marriages, it has its good times, not so good times, and some downright nasty times. God even "divorces" Israel for its unfaithfulness. In spite of this, God has promised reconciliation and restoration to the country.

When I got into this study and exploring this particular title, I almost decided to leave it out. There are some connotations to this word which many people disagree with today. I could tell you, but it's more fun for you find that out and draw out your own applications.

I will give you a spoiler to get you started. Like many of the names we have explored, the word for husband is a verb.

Please complete the Word Study for H1166.

What did you discover about this word?

Read Isaiah 54:1-10 and complete the Prophecy Summary for this passage.

How is Israel described in this passage?

What are the promises God makes to Israel

Have these promise been fulfilled? Explain your answer.

Isaiah refers to God several different ways. Make a note how each name would relate to God being a husband. If you have been working through this series of studies, you will discover you have explored most of them. Some might even appear as lessons or reviews this study guide.

Name	Meaning	Relation to Husband
Maker (H6213)		
LORD of Hosts (H3068, H6635)		
Redeemer (H1350)		
Holy One of Israel (H6918, H3478)		
God of the whole earth (H430, H3605, H776)		
LORD (H3068)		
God (H430)		

God through Isaiah compares this situation with promises made to Noah. What were those promises?

Has God kept them?

What are the promises He makes to Israel?

If God has kept His promise to Noah, what do you think the chances are He will keep His promises to Israel? Explain your answer.

If we carry to logic of God keeping His promises, what can we conclude about the promises which are applicable to us?

In verses eight and 10 God refers to His kindness (H2617) and mercy (H7355). We won't explore these words in depth but I have included Strong's number here for you. Write down a brief meaning and how they would refer to God as a husband.

Kindness:

Mercy:

Complete the My Name Is Chart.

What did you learn about God in this lesson?

Complete the following phrase.

God is a husband for the following reasons.

Word Summary Date of Study:

Word:	Verse:
Strong's Number:	

Definition:

Times Used:

Other Sources	Definition(s)

Other Bible References	How Used

Putting it My Own Words

Takeaway

Prophecy

Date of Study:

Passage:	Title:
Speaker:	Audience
Fulfilled? ☐ yes ☐ no when Fulfilled:	Thesis:

Literal:		Support

Figures/Symbols	Represents	Support

Passage in Context:

Purpose(s) of the Prophecy:

Takeaway:

My Name Is: Date:

First Mention:	Title:
Strong's #:	**Definition:**
Times Used:	

Other Sources	Notes/Definitions

Scripture	How Used	Support

Insight

Takeaway

Additional Notes:

The Name of the Lord is...

Room Nawsaw – The High and Lofty One

When I started to explore this title for God I was positive I had seen it before – well, at least part of it. The last time I (and hopefully you) explored Nawsaw it was in conjunction with Elohim and had been translated as the God-who-forgives.

It appears Nawsaw is one of those all-purpose words that can mean a lot of different things. So one of the things I wanted to know was why was it translated differently here?

It also turns out the word *room* is also a fairly versatile world and is used in a variety of ways. I would share them with you, but that would take away some of the wonders and questions you will have when you explore them.

I should also add a teeny, tiny bit of information. This may not be a title of God at all, but a reference to His physical position and worthiness to be exalted or worshipped. But then we've studied a few names which may fall in that same category. Depending on the version you are using it could go either way. I'll leave that for you to decide.

Complete the Déjà vu review for Nawsaw to refresh your memory about this word.

Now complete the Word Summary for H7311.

Read Isaiah 57:14-21 and complete the Prophecy Summary for this passage.

What is the context of the promises God is making in this passage?

How is God described?

Take a closer look at verse 15 by completing the Verse Summary.

Where does the passage say God Dwells?

How does the second word translated *high* differ from the first one?

The Name of the Lord is…

With whom does God dwell?

What is the English meaning of the word *contrite*?

What is the Hebrew meaning?

What does this say about the attitude of a person with this kind of heart?

Going through this passage again, record your findings on the God Is/Does Chart.

What did you learn about the High and Lofty One?

Complete the My Name Is Chart.

Complete the following sentence.

I bow the knee to the High and Lofty one who has promised…

Déjà vu Review		
Lofty One = Forgives		
Strong's #: H5375	Word:	Definition:
Verses:		
The Name of the Lord is…Vol. 2 page 141		
What did I discover about this name?		

Word Summary   Date of Study:

Word:	Verse:	
Strong's Number:		
Definition:		
Times Used:		
Other Sources	**Definition(s)**	
Other Bible References	**How Used**	
Putting it My Own Words		
Takeaway		

Prophecy

Date of Study:

Passage:	Title:
Speaker:	Audience
Fulfilled? ☐ yes ☐ no when Fulfilled:	Thesis:

Literal:		Support

Figures/Symbols	Represents	Support

Passage in Context:

Purpose(s) of the Prophecy:

Takeaway:

Verse Summary

Date of Study:

Title:	
Verse:	
Strong's Number and Definition(s)	**Used Elsewhere**
Quotation? Yes No	**Summary of Original Passage**

Summary of Verse in Context

Putting it in My Own Words

Takeaway

God Is/Does

Reference	Description	What do I think it means?	Support

My Name Is: Date:

First Mention:	Title:

Strong's #:

Times Used:

Definition:

Other Sources	Notes/Definitions

Scripture	How Used	Support

Insight

Takeaway

Additional Notes:

Déjà vu Review

Most High			
Strong's #: H5945	Word:	Definition:	

Verses:
Psalm 8:2

The Name of the Lord is: Vol. 2 – page 35
What did I discover about this name?

Awb – Father

We have a very different relationship with God than our counterparts had in the Old Testament. We are encouraged to call God our Father. We saw the special relationship of Father and Son through the example of Jesus Christ. We have free access to our heavenly Father because of the finished work of the cross.

Old Testament saints were familiar with God Most High, The Almighty and YAWEH. They held God in Awe and fear because they viewed Him as a powerful being who held their lives in His hands

Access to God was limited in the Old Testament to the High Priest, and then he was only permitted to enter the Holy of Holies to sprinkle blood on the Ark of the Covenant once a year. If you lived then and wanted to worship God, you were required to bring a sacrifice to the temple where a priest would take it, kill it and burn it for you.

Although the father – child relationship existed in the Old it was rarely stated as such. But it was still evident.

Let's begin our study by recording a few thoughts on what you think a father is.

Complete the Word Summary for H1

Read Isaiah 63 and complete the Poetry Summary for this passage.

What is the purpose of this prayer?

God is pictured as the Father of whom or what?

Why do you think this relationship would be highlighted in this passage?

What other names are used to identify God in this passage?

The Name of the Lord is...

Based on the context of the passage, why do you think Isaiah used these names and titles?

Look up the following references and record your findings on the God Is/Does chart

Exodus 4:22-23   Deuteronomy 32:6   I Chronicles 29:10   Isaiah 1:2
Isaiah 64:8   Jeremiah 3:19   Malachi 1:6   Malachi 2:10

How do these passages describe the relationship between God and Israel?

How is the father – child relationship different for people of the Old Testament and those of the New?

How is it the same?

Complete the My Name Is chart.

What did you learn about God the Father from your study?

Finish this thought:

God is my father and worthy of my worship

Word Summary

Date of Study:

Word:	Verse:
Strong's Number:	
Definition:	
Times Used:	

Other Sources	Definition(s)

Other Bible References	How Used

Putting it My Own Words

Takeaway

Poetry Summary

Date of Study:

Passage	Title:
Historical Context:	

Historical Context:

Verse:	Images:	Support

Insight from the Context:

Insight from Other Scripture or Sources	Source

Takeaway:

God Is/Does

Reference	Description	What do I think it means?	Support

My Name Is:

Date:

First Mention:	Title:
Strong's #:	Definition:
Times Used:	

Other Sources	Notes/Definitions

Scripture	How Used	Support

Insight

Takeaway

Additional Notes:

Déjà vu Review		
Redeemer		
Strong's #: 1350	Word:	Definition:
Verses:		
Psalm 19:14		
Psalm 78:35		
Isaiah 63:16		
The Name of the Lord is... Volume 3: The Great I Am		
What did I discover about this name?		

Ateek Yome – Ancient of Days

When putting together a Bible study of this scope what to include or exclude from the lessons sometimes becomes a judgment call. Take this name for instance. Depending on the commentator it could be a reference to Christ or to God. So the first question to decide was to include in this series or to set it aside for a future one dedicated to the names of Christ.

There are many references in the Old Testament to Jesus. He said as much when He spoke to the two disciples on the road to Emmaus (Luke 24:25-27). The Bible the Apostles and disciples used was what we consider our Old Testament. The New Testament as we know it was written before the end of the first century, but it wouldn't take the form we have today for another 200 years.

Although the argument can be made for both, the context of the passage seems to support this is referring to the Father. Unless someone can present some compelling arguments, this is where this name's home is.

Please complete the Word Summaries for H6268 and H3118

Please read Daniel 7:9-23 and complete the Prophecy Summary.

What is the context of this passage?

How is the Ancient of Days described?

What does the imagery suggest about the role He plays in this vision?

What evidence does the passage provide to indicate this name is in reference to God (the Father) and not to Jesus?

The Name of the Lord is...

What does this passage indicate about the responsibilities of the Ancient of Days?

Is or are there parallel passages in the Old or New Testament which are similar to this one?

List them here.

Are there any parallels between this word and the other names or titles we've looked at?

What are those names?

If we read through the entire chapter what is the major part of this vision about? (hint Daniel 7:26-27)

Complete the My Name is Chart.

What did you discover about the Ancient of Days which added to your understanding of who God is and what He does?

How would you finish this sentence?

I bow my knee to Ateek Yome, The Ancient of Days who is...

Word Summary

Date of Study:

Word:	Verse:
Strong's Number:	

Definition:

Times Used:

Other Sources	Definition(s)

Other Bible References	How Used

Putting it My Own Words

Takeaway

Prophecy

Date of Study:

Passage:	Title:
Speaker:	Audience
Fulfilled? ☐ yes ☐ no when Fulfilled:	Thesis:

Literal:	Support

Figures/Symbols	Represents	Support

Passage in Context:

Purpose(s) of the Prophecy:

Takeaway:

My Name Is: Date:

First Mention:	Title:	
Strong's #:	Definition:	
Times Used:		
Other Sources	**Notes/Definitions**	

Scripture	How Used	Support

Insight

Takeaway

Additional Notes:

Déjà vu Review

O Most Upright = Saviour		
Strong's #: 3477	Word:	Definition:

Verses:
Isaiah 26:7

The Name of the Lord is Vol.2 page 67
What did I discover about this name?

Works Cited

Baker, Warren. Carpenter, Eugene. *The Complete Word Study Dictionary: Old Testament*. Chattanooga: AMG Publishers, 2003.

—. *The Complete Word Study Dictionary; Old Testament*. Chatanooga: AMG Publishers, 2003.

dictionary.com. *Dictionary.com http://dictionary.reference.com/browse/superlative*. n.d. "superlative." Dictionary.com Unabridged. Random House, Inc. 27 Jul. 2015.

http://www.dictionary.com/browse/serendipity?s=t. n.d. 26 07 2016.

Lockyer, Herbert. *All the Divine Names and Titles in the Bible*. London: Pickering and Inglis Ltd., 1975.

Owens-Collins, Jamie. "The Battle Belongs to the Lord." Fair Hill Music, 1985.

And in Conclusion...

I haven't written a concluding chapter for several studies now. One of the reasons I decided not to write one is it didn't seem necessary. Most of the time they were reviews of the material we just finished exploring. Also during this particular series I changed the review process so it was scattered throughout the last two volumes and the choice was left up to you on whether you wanted to look at them.

If you have been with me throughout this series, we have explored 65 names and titles of God used in the Old Testament as well as an additional 20 lessons on what the Bible has to say about the name of God. This has also been a non-standard study as most are designed to be completed in a quarter, or 13 Lessons.

These ones have ranged from 15 to twenty lessons. I suppose a little bit of rearranging could have accommodated that standard by creating six and half books exploring the names instead of these five.

Six books are not a problem to design and write – it's that half book that would have been the challenge. Do I format it 4x10 or 8x5? Besides I have planned at least one more study in this series based on the New Testament.

In the introduction to the previous four books I made a point of mentioning my mentor Gary who would start the meetings at our college fellowship with by saying, "A relationship begins with a name."

I could ask you questions like "What is your favorite name and why?" or "Which of the names you've studied impacted you the most? And make you write down your answers.

The question I am going to leave with you is this: How has your concept of God, attitude towards God and relationship with God changed as a result of this study and series?

God bless you in your continued spiritual journey.

About the Author

Hi, I'm the author *of The Bible School Dropout's Bigger and Better Guide to Bible Study, The Bible School Dropout's Guide to More Bible Study, Xtreme Xianity, Core Elements, In Hot Pursuit* and The Name of the Lord is series. I am also the author of the novels *Free* and *Icthus.*

These Bible studies are based upon inductive Bible study methods which use grammatical-historical, normal or literal methods of interpretation. If you can ask the questions; who, what, where, why, when and how, then you can do an inductive Bible study.

I really am a Bible school dropout. I left Bible school at the beginning of my third year. But that was not the end of my Christian experience and I have been actively teaching and writing study material for over 30 years.

It doesn't matter if you have had formal training or not. Anyone with the right tools and practice can study their Bible for themselves. I encourage people to learn how to study their Bibles and learn what it has to say instead of letting others tell them what it says.

Feedback and suggestions are welcome. Drop a line to bibleschooldropout@gmail.com. You can also visit my website www.bibleschooldropout.com.

Learn More about Inductive Bible Study

If you enjoyed this study and want to learn more about inductive Bible study, I encourage you to pick up my books (preferably) on doing just that.

They are available through my website www.bibleschooldropout.com and on Amazon. *The Bible School Dropout's Gide to Building the Word of God in my Life* is also available as a free e-book download on Smashwords.com.

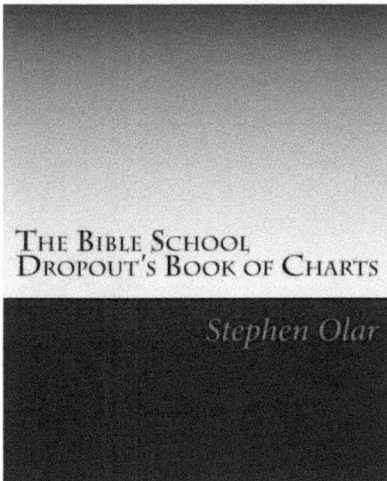

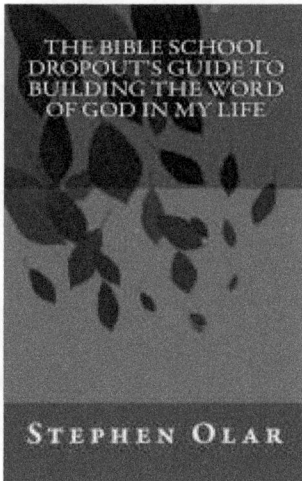

THE BIBLE SCHOOL DROPOUT'S BIGGER AND BETTER GUIDE TO BIBLE STUDY
Stephen Olar

THE BIBLE SCHOOL DROPOUT'S GUIDE TO MORE BIBLE STUDY
Stephen Olar

THE BIBLE SCHOOL DROPOUT'S BOOK OF CHARTS
Stephen Olar

THE BIBLE SCHOOL DROPOUT'S GUIDE TO BUILDING THE WORD OF GOD IN MY LIFE
STEPHEN OLAR

The Name of the Lord is...

www.ingramcontent.com/pod-product-compliance
Lightning Source LLC
Chambersburg PA
CBHW052341100426
42736CB00046B/3261